AF395186

Published in 2024 by:

Northern Eye Books Limited
Northern Eye Books, Tattenhall, Cheshire CH3 9PX
© Northern Eye Books Limited 2024

ISBN 978-1-914589-20-1

Text: *Carl Rogers*

Photographs: *Carl Rogers, Shutterstock, Dreamstime*

Design: *Carl Rogers and Laura Hodgkinson*

Carl Rogers has asserted his rights under the Copyright, Designs and Patents Act, 1988 to be identified as the author of this work. All rights reserved

A CIP catalogue record for this book is available from the British Library.

Printed in the EU by Latitude on woodland-friendly FSC stock

www.northerneyebooks.co.uk

 @northerneyebooks
@carlrogers1960

 @northerneyeboo
@CarlMaraBooks

 @northerneyebooks

For sales enquiries, please call 01928 723 744
tony@northerneyebooks.co.uk

Important Advice: The routes described in this book are undertaken at the reader's own risk. Walkers should take into account their level of fitness, wear suitable footwear and clothing, and carry food and water. It is also advisable to take the relevant OS map with you in case you get lost and leave the area covered by our maps.

Whilst every care has been taken to ensure the accuracy of the route directions, the publishers cannot accept responsibility for errors or omissions, or for changes in the details given. Nor can the publisher and copyright owners accept responsibility for any consequences arising from the use of this book.

If you find any inaccuracies in either the text or maps, please write or email us at the address above. Thank you.

This book contains mapping data licensed from the Ordnance Survey with the permission of the Controller of Her Majesty's Stationery Office. © Crown copyright 2023 All rights reserved. License number 100047867

Cover: *Wasdale Head Inn (Walk 10).*
Photo: Carl Rogers

Contents

Cockermouth
Bassenthwaite Lake
Skiddaw
Blencathra
M6
Penrith
A66
A66
Lorton
Keswick
Braithwaite
Grisedale Pike
Loweswater
Derwent Water
Crummock Water
Buttermere
Borrowdale
Glenridding
Ullswater
Helvellyn
Patterdale
Ennerdale Water
Buttermere
Haweswater
Ennerdale
Thirlmere
Fairfield
Great Gable
A591
High Street
Langdale Pikes
Wasdale
Scafell Pike
Scafell
Grasmere
Bowfell
Langdale
Wast Water
Ambleside
Troutbeck
Eskdale
Windermere
Windermere
Old Man of Coniston
Hawkshead
Coniston

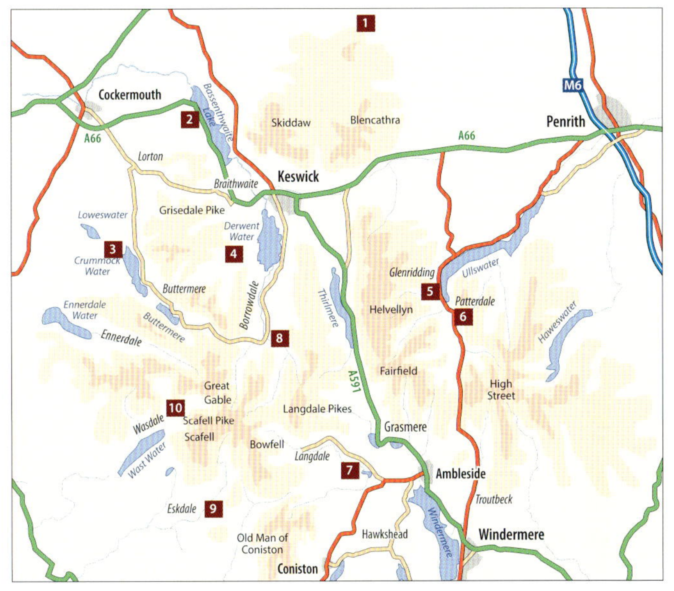

England's Largest National Park

THE LAKE DISTRICT NATIONAL PARK is the largest and most popular of the thirteen National Parks in England and Wales. Created as one of Britain's first National Parks in 1951, its role is to 'conserve and enhance' the natural beauty, wildlife and culture of this iconic English landscape, not just for residents and visitors today but for future generations, too.

Remarkably, the National Park contains every scrap of England's land over 3,000 feet, including its highest mountain, Scafell Pike. Packed within the Park's 885 square miles are numerous peaks and fells, over 400 lakes and tarns, around 50 dales, six National Nature Reserves, and more than 100 Sites of Special Scientific Interest—all publicly accessible on over 1,800 miles of footpaths and other rights of way. It's no surprise then, that the Lake District attracts an estimated 15 million visitors a year.

Grange, Borrowdale

Pub and fell walks

The Lake District boasts some of Britain's best traditional pubs and some of its loveliest mountains, hills and fells. So, imagine if you could combine the two for the perfect day or half day out. By happy coincidence, there are a few places where a perfect pub lies close to a famous fell.

Here are ten carefully-chosen circular walks that combine an iconic lakeland fell with a nearby Cumbrian pub or inn. With the help of this handy little book, you can now enjoy a superb fell walk with a drink and maybe some food in the relaxed surroundings of a traditional Cumbrian country pub.

"There is nothing which has yet been contrived by man, by which so much happiness is produced as by a good tavern."

Samuel Johnson

TOP 10 **Walks:** Pubs and fells

THE TEN WALKS IN THIS BOOK combine superb natural pairings of a great Lakeland pub with a circular walk on a neighbouring fell. What could be better than a bracing fell walk followed by a pint and some food in a traditional Cumbrian pub or inn? Enjoy honest exercise, wonderful views and a sense of achievement before rewarding yourself with a relaxing drink in cosy, welcoming surroundings. Up hill and down the pub—what more could you want?—the perfect combination!

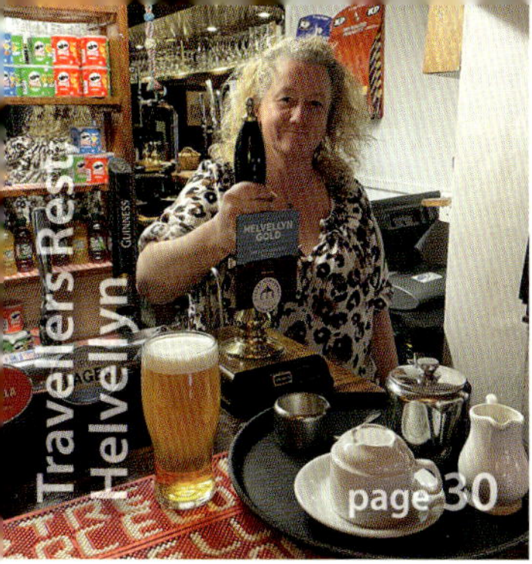

Travellers Rest, Helvellyn
page 30

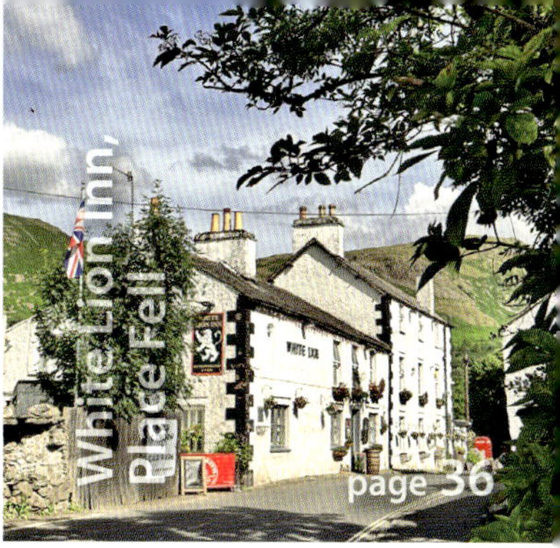

White Lion Inn, Place Fell
page 36

The Britannia Inn, Lingmoor Fell
page 40

The Riverside Bar, Grange Pike
page 46

Woolpack Inn, Harter Fell
page 52

Wasdale Head Inn, Scafell Pike
page 58

The Old Crown, Hesket Newmarket

The Old Crown | High Pike
Hesket Newmarket

Distance/time: 16km / 10 miles. Allow 4½ hours

Start: Small car park in the centre of Heskett Newmarket

Grid ref: NY 342 386

Ordnance Survey Map: OL5 The English Lakes North-Eastern area, *Penrith, Patterdale & Caldbeck*

The Pub: The Old Crown, Hesket Newmarket, Wigton CA7 8JG | 016974 78288 | www.theoldcrownpub.co.uk

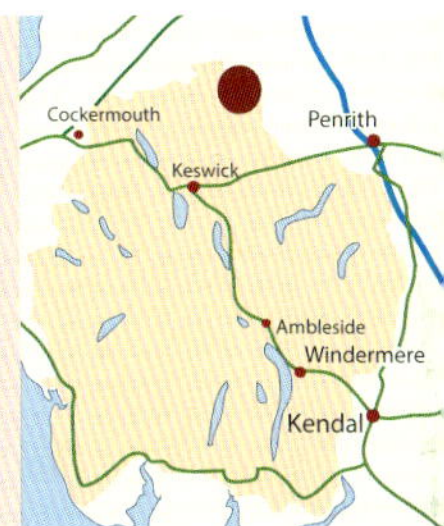

Walk outline: Beginning in the small village of Hesket Newmarket, this walk uses old farm lanes to access the open fell. Straightforward walking over open ground leads onto the broad ridge connecting Carrock Fell and High Pike. Easy walking over grassy open fell, before a gradual descent and return using farm track and quiet lanes.

The Old Crown is England's first co-operatively owned pub and sits at the heart of the attractive Cumbrian village of Heskett Newmarket. It was bought by 125 locals in 2003 to save it from either closure or being swallowed up by larger breweries and is now the subject of real local pride.

▶ The Old Crown at a glance

Open: Mon–Fri 5pm–10pm, Sat & Sun 12noon–10.30pm
Brewery/company: Free house,
Real ales: A selection of local ales including the Hesket Newmarket Brewery (situated adjacent to the pub)
Food: Evenings Tuesday to Saturday. Sunday luch and evenings. Take away menu also available. Orders can be made by phone.
Rooms: No accommodation available
Outside: Tables at the front of the pub and undercover seating to rear
Children & dogs: Children and dogs on leads welcome

The Walk

1. Facing the pub, go right through the village passing the **community shop and Post Office**. Where the road swings right take the lane ahead (left). Take the lane on the left almost immediately. This lane rises gently with Carrock Fell rising directly ahead.

2. The lane eventually passes **Wood Hall**, a large, well kept hill farm. Immediately after the **outbuildings**, look for a signed footpath on the right. Go through the lage field gate and pass a **small pool** on the left to reach a stile in the far fence. Cross the stile into a large grazing field and aim to the right of a distant **conifer wood**. As you rise through the field look for a large ladder stile in the **high stone wall** ahead, about 200 metres to the right of the conifer wood.

3. Go over the stile onto the open fell. Cross a small stream almost immediately and turn left to follow an obvious path parrallel to the wall on the left. A little further on, cross a larger beck (**Blea Gill**) flowing down from the mine remains up to the right, and continue ahead parallel to the wall.

Eventually the path reaches a **prominent track**. Turn left along the track for around 100 metres or so, then bear right heading diagonally up the fellside to reach a contouring footpath visible above.

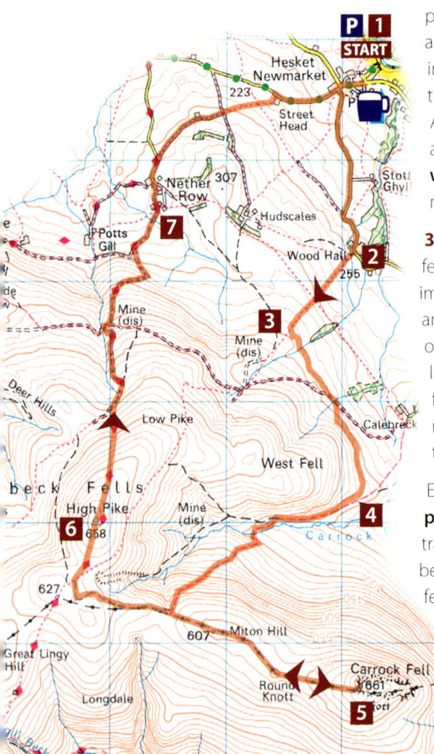

Turn left along the path and follow it past **fenced mine openings**. The path contours the hillside eventually curving right into the valley of **Carrock Beck**. A number of paths join from the left but keep going until you meet the **wide track** that aims for the valley head with the beck down to the left.

4. Turn right along the track heading directly up the valley. In around ½ mile/750 metres the path splits. The more prominent path continues ahead and a narrower grassy path breaks left. Bear left here soon crossing the **beck** to

climb more steeply to the rounded ridge above where you meet a good footpath.

To include **Carrock Fell** turn left and follow the path along the broad ridge —a series of rocky knolls separated by boggy hollows. It is about 1½ miles/2 kilometres each way.

Carrock Fell is a great viewpoint in clear conditions with views across the rolling Northern Fells to Skiddaw and Blencathra as well as east across the Eden Valley and north to the Scottish Lowlands.

5. Retrace your route along the ridge passing the ascent path and keep ahead

Looking southeast from Carrock Fell into the Northern Fells

until you see a path curving right across the head of **Drygill Beck** towards the summit of **High Pike**.

Bear right along this path keeping ahead at a prominent crossing track, and following it to the summit cairn.

6. From the summit of High Pike head due north (towards the tall mast) passing a stone wind shelter, then continue with the village of **Caldbeck** down in the valley directly ahead. A more promising looking footpath veers to the right here, but ignore it keeping ahead. This path follows the **Cumbria Way** down to **Nether Row Farm**.

Where the angle eases you meet a crossing path. Turn right here and shortly after **mining spoil** stay with the main path (ignore a less obvious path ahead) as it swings left down the hillside. Pass through more mining remains keeping ahead at a crossing track and staying with the most obvious path ahead which eventually becomes a 4x4 track.

7. Leave the open fellside at a gate signed to **Claybottom Farm**. Follow the track passing through the yard between the house and outbuildings. Follow the access track to reach a lane end at Nether Row Farm.

Follow the lane for around 250 metres turn right onto a signed footpath.Initially the path follows a farm track between fields. At a junction take the path ahead eventually running into fields. Go ahead through the field towards a **house**. Keep to the left of the house to enter a lane. Turn right and follow the lane back to Hesket Newmarket to complete the walk. ◆

Centuries of mining

The northern fells are rich in mineral deposits thought to have been worked as far back as the 12th century, although documented evidence only goes back to the reign of Elizabeth I when German miners were brought in. The workings reached a peak around the 1820s with the majority closed by the end of the century. Today the area is highly regarded by mineral and crystal collectors, but removal of samples is strictly controlled.

The Pheasant, Wythop

The Pheasant | Sale Fell Wythop

Quiet lanes; low-lying grassy fell; woodland tracks

Distance/time: 5km / 3 miles. Allow 1½–2 hours

Start: There is room for a few cars in a loop of the old main road close to the pub

Grid ref: NY 200 307

Ordnance Survey Map: OL7 The English Lakes North-western area, *Keswick, Cockermouth & Wigton*

The Pub: The Pheasant, Bassenthwaite Lake, Cockermouth, Cumbria CA13 9YE | 01768 776234 | www.the-pheasant.co.uk | reception@the-pheasant.co.uk

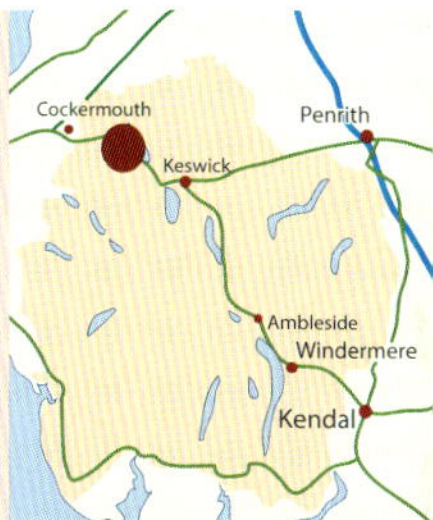

Walk outline: Beginning in a loop of the old A66, the walk heads along a quiet lane before striking out across the open fell with widening views. The grassy ascent to Sale Fell's summit is quickly over and its modest summit gives surprisingly good views across Bassenthwaite Lake to the great bulk of Skiddaw. Return is made by straightfoward forest tracks. An ideal half-day walk.

Originating as a 17th-century coaching inn, The Pheasant has been carefully refurbished to retain much of its original character. The rooms are relaxing and cozy and a range of local ales and excellent food make for a perfect end to your walk.

Hand-painted inn sign

▶ The Pheasant at a glance

Open: Daily 8am–9pm, pub 10am–11pm daily

Brewery/company: The Inn Collection Group

Real ales: Hand-pulled and cask ales, bitters and lagers including Loweswater Gold

Food: Local Cumbrian produce is used to create a range of tasty dishes with a seasonal menu, children's menu and special Sunday roasts. Lunchtime snacks and sandwiches

Outside: Patio area with tables to the rear of the hotel

Children & dogs: Children welcome. Dog friendly

The Walk

1. Facing the **Pheasant Inn** go right and at the end of the buildings, turn left into the lane signed to 'Wythop Mill 1½'. Walk up the lane, soon becoming steeper, then more gentle as it swings right.

2. In about 1 kilometre/¾ mile, look for a signed footpath ('Public footpath Kelswick') on the left. There are often cars parked on the verge here. Through the gate, the obvious footpath climbs steadily between gorse bushes at first, then after a gap in the **wall**, continues over the open grassy fell with widening views.

The path levels by a **well-built wall** on the right on the crest of the broad rounded ridge. Take the path which breaks left here and follow this gradually all the way to the **summit**—a broad grassy dome with wide views to Wythop Woods, the Whinlatter fells and across Bassenthwaite to Skiddaw.

3. From the summit, head down to a broad grassy saddle (in the direction of Skiddaw) to pass through a **gateway** in the wall. Go straight ahead now to a **cairn** on the skyline. From the cairn a footpath follows the grassy skyline ridge to a second summit where there is a **memorial bench**.

4. Continue along the **grassy ridge** towards a **wall** visible ahead. Just before the wall bear right for a few metres, then turn sharp right onto a footpath beside **oak trees**. This path soon swings left down to reach a T junction. Turn

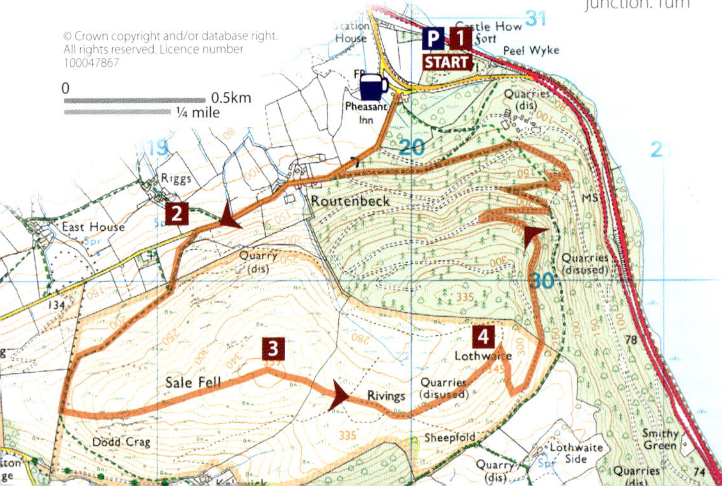

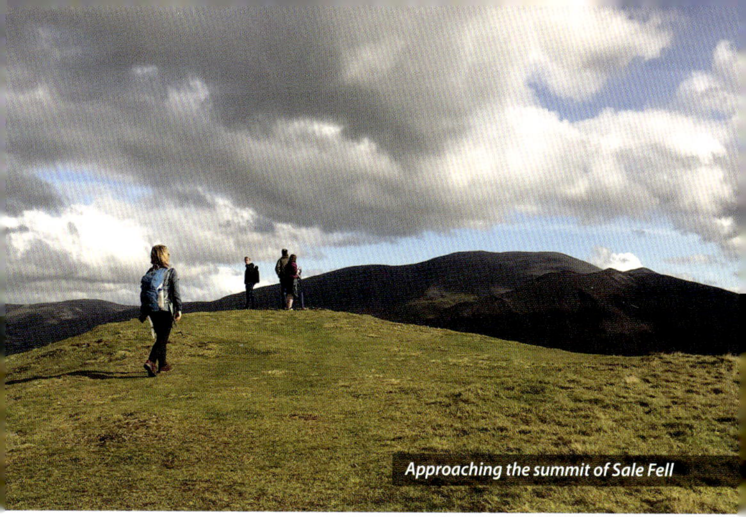
Approaching the summit of Sale Fell

left here and shortly enter **woods** through a large gate.

Follow a good path ahead and keep right at the first fork. Follow a forest track down to a T junction, turn right and continue the descent. Stay with the main track as it turns sharp left (ignore a right). At the next junction turn sharp-right zig-zagging down to another T junction.

Turn left here, soon with **forestry buildings** down to the right. Where the track turns sharp right, keep ahead on a footpath and follow it to the lane. Turn right to return to the The Pheasant to complete the walk. ♦

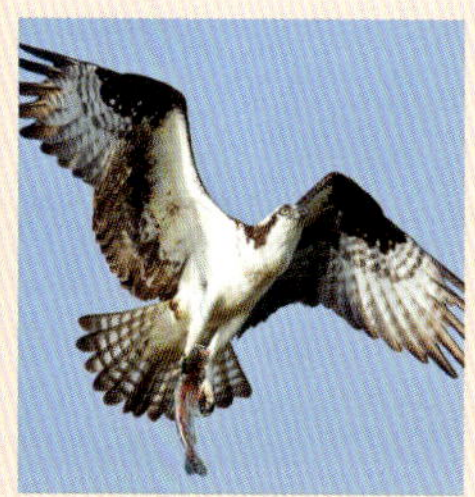

Ospreys

Ospreys are spectacular fish-eating birds of prey with a five-foot wingspan. In 2001, after an absence of 150 years, a pair returned to breed in the Lake District. They were encouraged by an artificial nesting platform overlooking Bassenthwaite Lake and they've returned to raise one or two chicks every year since. The ospreys can be watched through telescopes or binoculars from a staffed viewing platform at Dodd Wood.

The Kirkstile Inn and Mellbreak

Kirkstile Inn | Mellbreak
Loweswater

Distance/time: 11km / 6¾ miles. Allow 3½-4 hours

Start: National Trust car park at Scalehill Bridge, Loweswater. Fee required

Grid ref: NY 149 215

Ordnance Survey Map: OL 4 The English Lakes North-western area. *Keswick, Cockermouth & Wigton*

The Pub: Kirkstile Inn, Loweswater, Cumbria CA13 0RU | 01900 85219 | www.kirkstile.com | info@kirkstile.com

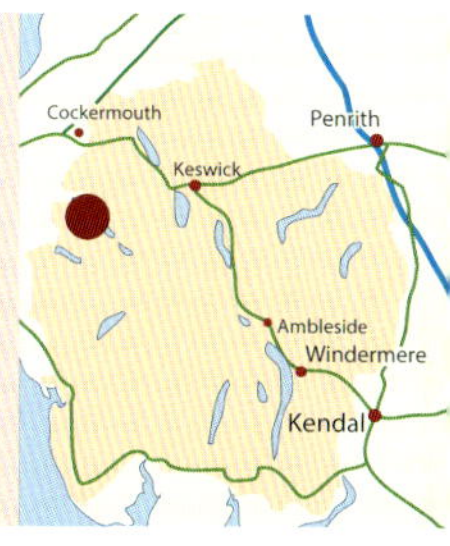

Walk outline: From the car park, quiet lanes lead past the hamlet of Loweswater with its church and pub before a steady climb towards Mellbreak. A steep climb is followed by some scrambling up Mellbreak's north ridge to reach the summit. Easy walking between the fell's two summits followed by a return along a beautiful lakeside path.

Tucked away between Loweswater and Crummock Water, the Kirkstile Inn is a classic Lakeland pub that has been providing food and shelter since Tudor times. Modern visitors can expect a relaxed atmosphere, low beams, open fires, good food and beer. There are two bars and a comfortable dining room.

▶ Kirkstile Inn at a glance

Open: Mon–Sat 11am–11pm; Sun 12noon–10.30pm
Brewery/company: Free house with own brewery
Real ales: Loweswater Gold, Melbreak bitter, Coniston Bluebird, Grasmoor Dark, Yates bitter, guest beers
Food: Daily 12noon–2pm, 6–9pm. Excellent, rustic dishes with a Cumbrian focus. Specials board. Often busy, booking advisable
Rooms: Four rooms en-suite, plus family annexe
Outside: Lovely beer garden with 20 tables and a play area
Children & dogs: Children welcome. Dogs allowed in bar only

The Walk

1. Turn left out of the car park and follow the lane. Keep ahead at the crossroads but turn left at the next lane in around 500 metres signed to the '**Kirkstile Inn**'.

2. The pub sits at the end of the lane opposite **Loweswater church** with a great view out over the fields to Grasmoor. Resist the temptation for a quick pint, turning left immediately before the pub and take the first lane on the right almost immediately.

Follow the lane which, beyond **Kirkhead Farm**, becomes a rougher, unsurfaced farm track.

Mellbreak rises directly ahead now and looks quite dramatic for such a modest fell, even in the shadow of Grasmoor its giant neighbour.

3. Where the track swings right immediately below woods, there is a gate and the track splits. Take the path up through the wood. The path emerges on the open lower slopes of **Mellbreak** and a narrow footpath heads directly towards the steep northern spur of the fell. Take this path and follow it as it quickly gains height, finally zig-zaging up steepening scree.

[**An easier option** avoiding any scrambling is to continue ahead where the track splits below the woods following the track into and along Mosedale for about 1.5km. A path breaks left here to reach the summit plateau at its mid point.]

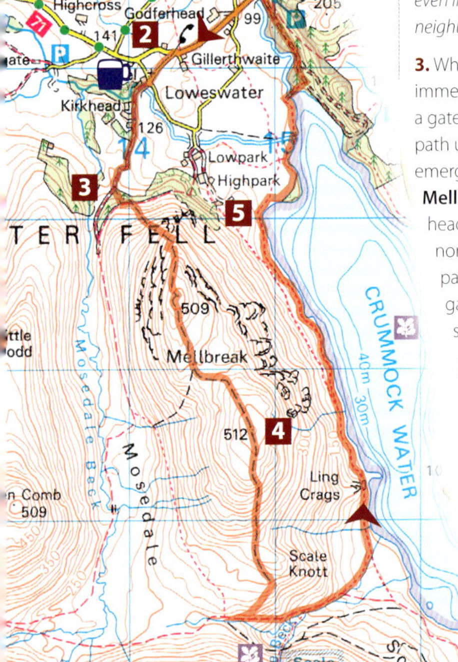

Spectacular 'birds eye' view of Crummock Water

Above the scree, the path crosses loose broken rocks where care is needed and you will need the occasional steadying hand here and there.

As the path climbs it moves over to the northern spur of the fell and passes close to a **deep gully** on the left. Again, care is needed here and it may not be suitable for anyone not keen on heights as there is some mild exposure here. *If you enjoy situations like this, you will love the spectacular views looking directly down to the Kirkstile Inn and the cottages of Lowpark and Highpark directly below.*

The climb continues over easier ground, mainly scree and heather, to eventually reach the northern summit at 509 metres.

Despite its modest height and lofty neighbours, Mellbreak is a superb viewpoint.

A broad path heads south across the substantial **summit plateau**, which can be surprisingly boggy at times. At the broad saddle on the ridge midway between the two summits the easier option joins from the right.

The spectacular view from the steep northern spur of Mellbreak

4. The main summit is just three metres higher than the northern top, but also enjoys spectacular views, particularly up towards the head of the valley with Buttermere lake and the shapely Fleetwith Pike prominent.

A grassy path heads down the southern slopes, becoming steeper as it descends. Over the small subsidiary top of **Scale Knott** the path curves rightwards before descending to join the broad path beside **Black Beck**. Turn left along this path keeping above the beck.

Stay to the left of the beck and stone walls to the right and ignore a footbridge on the right. Eventually you will reach the shore of **Crummock Water** close to the little shingle peninsula of **Low Ling Crag**.

A good path follows the shore of the lake below the steep eastern face of Mellbreak.

This is a lovely stretch of path, often quiet and with superb views across to the massive western face of Grasmoor, rising an amazing 700 metres above Crummock Water.

There is a beautiful shingle beach in about 2 kilometres with a classic view back up the valley to the High Stile range and

Rannerdale Knotts—arguambly one of the finest views in the Lake District.

5. Beyond the shingle beach the path hugs the lake shore eventually crossing footbridges over the outflow in **Llanthwaite Wood**. Take the path left into the woods behind the **benches** and follow this back to the car park to complete the route. ◆

Wild swimming?

What could be lovelier on a hot summer's day than sliding into the cool waters of a mountain stream, river pool or lake? Swimming in crystal clear waters surrounded by lofty fells is a real delight. For those in the know, the pebble 'beaches' at the top end of Crummock Water are one of the Lake District's finest and most easily accessible wild swimming spots.

The Swinside Inn and Causey Pike

The Swinside Inn | Causey Pike
Newlands

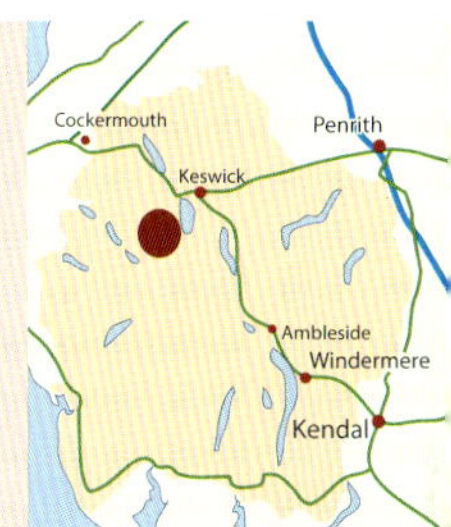

Distance/time: 8.5km / 5¼ miles. Allow 3–3½ hours

Start: Layby parking below Barrow near Uzzicar and Stoneycroft. Alternative start could be made from Rigg Beck Bridge, or a small car park at Stair. The Swinside Inn is off the route along the lane beyond Stair.

Grid ref: NY 233 217

Ordnance Survey Map: OL 4 The English Lakes North-western area. *Keswick, Cockermouth & Wigton*

The Pub: The Swinside Inn, Newlands Valley, Keswick CA12 5UE | 017687 78253 | www. swinsideinn.co.uk |

Walk outline: The climbing starts immediately on this walk heading steeply up the northern flanks of Causey Pike followed by a final narrowing of the ridge to reach the summit. An enjoyable ridge leads to Scar Crags with a descent and reascent to reach the shapely edge of Ard Crags. The ridge crest is followed back down into the valley with a return along the lane from Rigg Beck bridge.

Originally three 17th-century miner's cottages, The Swinside Inn is a traditional family-run Lakeland pub serving good food and local ales. With some of the best beer garden views in the Lake District, it makes a perfect end to your day on the fells.

▶ The Swinside Inn at a glance

Open: Mon-Sat, 11am–11pm; Sun, 11am–10.30pm;

Brewery/company: Free house

Real ales: Three regular real ales including Theakston Lightfoot

Food: Daily, lunches 12noon–5pm, 5.30–8.30pm; booking recommended

Rooms: B&B accommodation available

Outside: Seating area with wide views of the Newland fells

Children & dogs: Children and dogs welcome

The Walk

1. From the large layby adjacent to **Uzzicar**, go left along the lane. Just beyond the **bridge** over the beck (**Stonycroft Gill**), take the signed footpath on the right. This climbs steadily above the beck with the shapely cone of **Causey Pike** rising ahead.

The climb is steep but steady. Ignore joining paths keeping on the main path directly ahead. This eventually swings left steepening a little more and finally zig-zaging to reach **Sleet Hause**, the saddle between **Rowling End** and Causey Pike.

The final climb of almost 200 metres is both steep and obvious and follows the fine-looking ridge above. The final few metres require simple scrambling and the use of your hands here and there, but there is nothing difficult and little or no exposure.

In clear conditions the summit views are magnificent. The fall into the Newlands valley will probably grab your attention first with its rolling green pastures contrasting so dramatically with the sweeping ridges of High Snab Bank on Robinson and Scope End on Hindscarth.

To the east you will see the northern end of Derwent Water glimpsed over the shoulder of the famous Catbells watched over by Skiddaw, one of the four Lakeland giants.

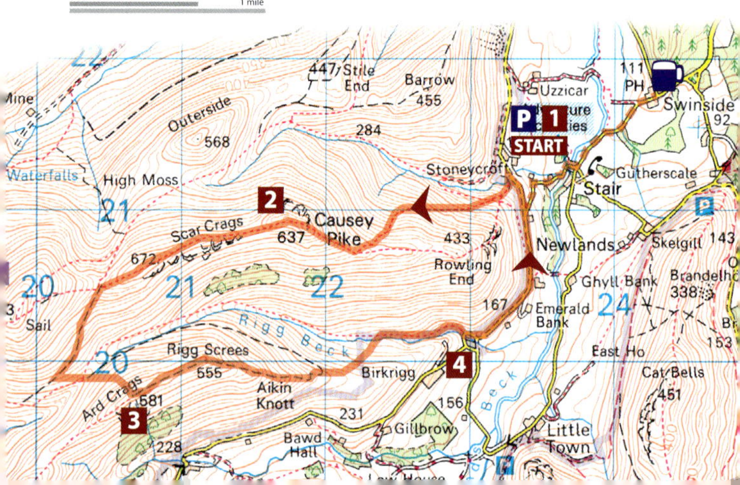

Looking towards Scar Crags from Causey Pike

To the west the view takes in the higher tops of the Derwent Fells: Grisedale Pike, Hopegill Head and Crag Hill.

2. From Causey Pike, the way is obvious following the ridge west towards **Scar Crags**. (At the first saddle the path on the right could be use to shorten the walk providing a quick descent to the path beside Stonycroft Gill).

This ridge is a delight, especially in clear conditions; the walking is easy, the ridge just narrow enough to be interesting and the views on either side magnificent.

At the next saddle you have a choice. Ahead you will have noticed the alarming 'new' path that has been constructed on the steep eastern flanks of Sail. This would take you on to the Grasmoor group and a much longer day. The path to the right leads down over High Moss and could be used take in the tops of Outerside and Barrow.

The reccommended route is to take the slightly less obvious path to the left. This drops into the impressive little valley separating Scar Crags from the striking grassy ridge of **Ard Crags**, which will

The stunning view to Robinson, Hindcarth and Newlands valley from Ard Crags

have caught your eye as you walked along the ridge from Causey Pike. The path cuts diagonally across the slope. Follow the path until you are directly above the highest point in the valley below and take the narrown path that drops directly to the saddle.

Take the faint footpath heading diagonally left up the steep northwestern slopes of Ard Crags.

Ard Crags is a great little summit, often empty when the more popular fells are crowded and offering superb views of the green vale of the Newlands Valley to Robinson and Hindscarth.

3. If you have the time and the inclination, it is worth the easy out-and-back detour to **Knott Rigg** at the southwestern end of the ridge. This offers great views into Newlands all the way along the ridge.

To continue from Ard Crags, head northeast along the ridge, which soon descends over **Aiken Knott**, then more steeply.

Where the angle eases, look for a signed footpath that veers half-left away from the ridge crest and cuts through the bracken towards **Rigg Beck**.

When you reach the beck, cross over and join the good footpath on the far bank. Follow this path beside the beck all the way down to the lane, where there is a little **parking area** by the bridge.

4. Turn left and follow the lane back to Stair. The Swinside Inn is half a mile up the lane from Stair. ♦

Buzzards

Once seldom seen in the UK, common buzzards are now Britain's most numerous birds of prey. These large brown birds of prey are most often spotted circling high above the Lakeland woods and fells. They can easily be recognised by their fanned tails and long rounded wings held in a shallow 'V'. Listen, too, for their distinctive mewling call—a repeated 'pee-oo', 'pee-oo'.

Travellers Rest, Glenridding

Travellers Rest | Helvellyn
Glenridding

Distance: 16km/10 miles. Allow 5–6hours

Start: Glenridding (Pay and Display) car park and toilets by the National Park Visitor Centre, in Glenridding Village

Grid ref: NY 385 169

Ordnance Survey Map: OL 5 *The English Lakes North-eastern area. Penrith, Patterdale & Caldbeck*

The Pub: Travellers Rest, 2 Greenside Rd, Glenridding, Penrith CA11 0QQ | 017684 82298 |

Walk outline: Starting at the National Park car park in Glenridding, this route gains height quickly with a steep ascent of Birkhouse Moor, with its wide views of the route ahead. An ascent of the famous scramblers' ridge Swirral Edge, will take you onto the broad summit plateau. The descent route is over easier ground via White Side and the Kepple Cove zig-zags, followed by an easy walk back along the rough valley road.

The Travellers Rest is a small traditional, two-roomed pub with open fires ideally situated to catch walkers returning from an ascent of Helvellyn.

▶ Travellers Rest at a glance

Open: Daily 11am–11pm

Brewery/company: Free house

Real ales: One regular beer, Hesket Newmarket Helvellyn Gold

Food: Daily lunches 12noon–2.30pm, evening 6pm–9.30pm

Rooms: No accommodation, camping nearby

Outside: Small outside seating area

Children & dogs: Children welcome and dog friendly

The Walk

1. Leave the car park at its far end, in the right-hand corner, on the signed path for 'Helvellyn'. Pass the **Health Centre**, on the left, and at the road (Greenside Road) turn left. Pass the '**Traveller's Rest**' and in around 150 metres take the lane on the left, signposted to '**Gillside Farm**'.

The lane drops to cross the river at **Rattlebeck Bridge**, then rises again. Just before the **farm**, bear right onto a rough unmetalled track. Ignore a right of way on the right keeping ahead through a gate on the rising track. Keep right at a **house** higher up to eventually reach a large gate onto the open fell.

Turn left immediately over a small **footbridge** to begin the climb beside the beck.

2. On the high shoulder of **Birkhouse Moor**, the angle eases a little as the footpath swings right and continues beside a **stone wall**.

Eventually you crest the ridge at almost 700 metres and are greeted by a superb panorama of the route ahead—from Helvellyn and Catstycam to Lower Man and Whiteside.

3. For Birkhouse Moor bear right for 200 metres or so but return to this point to continue. The path heads towards Helvellyn now parallel to the wall.

In just under a kilometer, you reach the famous '**Hole-in-the-Wall**' where stiles lead over the wall. Don't cross here, instead, bear right on the broad path that heads towards the unseen **Red Tarn**.

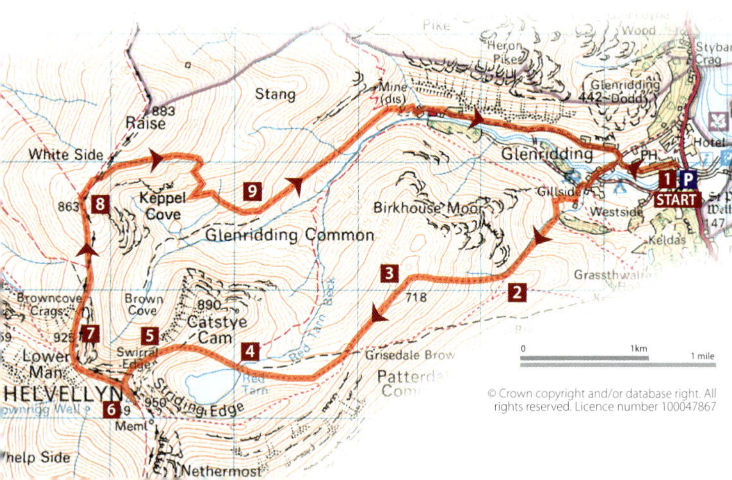

Looking towards Swirral Edge from Red Tarn

4. Cross **Red Tarn Beck** near the outflow where there is a junction of paths. Take the path ahead which climbs the southern slopes of **Catstycam**, to reach the saddle on the skyline ahead. [Catstycam is a straight forward out and back from here if you want to include it.]

Red Tarn, seen below, sits in a high, bowl-shaped valley known as a 'cirque'—formed during cold periods when snow accumulates to form a small glacier. The local name for these high valleys is 'cove'. Nearby examples include Keppel Cove, Brown Cove and Nethermost Cove.

The path on towards **Swirral Edge**, skirts the first rocks on the left to reach a level saddle before the main arête above.

5. Stay as close to the main ridge as you can following the clearly worn rocks. The ridge is a little exposed in places, particularly on the right, but any difficulties can be by-passed by easier ground on the left. The ridge leads directly onto the **Helvellyn plateau**.

6. Go left along the plateau edge, past the triangulation pillar, to reach the cairn on the **summit of Helvellyn**.

Red Tarn and Swirral Edge from the summit of Helvellyn

Helvellyn is one of the few Lakeland summits where almost every other fell is visible. The most striking panorama is to the west taking in the Coniston Fells, Bowfell, Esk Pike, Scafell Pike and Great Gable.

Retrace your steps to the top of Swirral Edge but don't go down the ridge —instead, follow the plateau edge descending gradually. When the path forks near a cairn, cut right, rising to the summit of **Lower Man**.

7. From Lower Man take the path north, descending over rough ground to a broad saddle. Cross the saddle, continuing in the same direction on the wide path to the cairn on the **summit of White Side**.

8. Continue along the ridge, descending northeast-wards, to reach another saddle between White Side and Raise. When the path forks, go right on a good path before you reach **Raise**. Follow the well-cairned route, continuing to descend the **Keppel Cove zig-zags**, with the old dam at the dry tarn below and the northwest ridge of Catstycam prominently in view. Drop down to reach a path coming in from the right.

9. Turn left on this path, walking towards **Sheffield Pike** and the **Greenside Mines**.

Just before the mine's spoil heaps, the track curves sharp right, then left. Descend towards the buildings below, curving to the right towards a gate. Go left past '**Almond Lodge**', and through a kissing gate. Walk between the buildings, past the **Youth Hostel**, and back down the access lane to return to **Glenridding** village via the Travellers Rest. Follow the outward route back to the car park to complete the walk. ♦

Ordnance Survey trig points

Like many Lakeland fells, Helvellyn is topped by a 'trig point'—or triangulation pillar. It's one of 6,500 erected across Britain by the Ordnance Survey to support accurate large-scale land surveying. These hilltop pillars acted as a solid base for surveying instruments called theodolites. Although the 'trig points' original role has gone, many remain on summits across the country as handy reference points in bad weather—often stumbled across by grateful walkers.

White Lion Inn, Patterdale

White Lion Inn | Place Fell
Patterdale

Distance/time: 5.5km / 3½ miles. Allow 3½–4 hours

Start: Small pay and display car park opposite the 'Patterdale Hotel', Patterdale.

Grid ref: NY 396 159

Ordnance Survey Map: OL 4 The English Lakes North-eastern area. *Penrith, Patterdale & Caldbeck*

The Pub: White Lion Inn, Patterdale, Penrith CA11 0NW | 017684 82214 | www.whitelionpatterdale.com | info@whitelionpatterdale.com

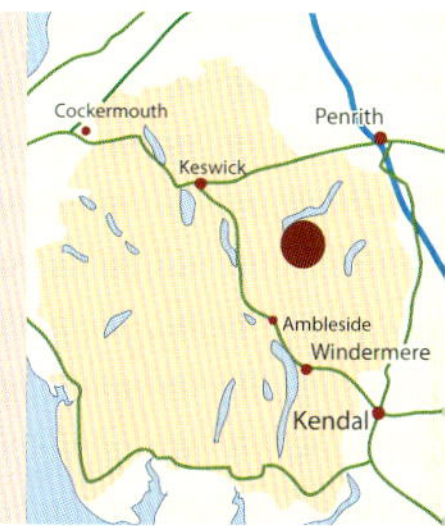

Walk outline: This walk offers an unusual approach to Place Fell—one of the best viewpoints in the north-eastern Fells. An attractive walk on the lakeside path from Patterdale is followed by a short steep climb to the summit with dramatic views back to Ullswater. The conventional route descending to Boredale Hause is used to return.

The White Lion Inn is an unusual country inn dating back to the early 1800s when, it is claimed, Wordsworth was in the bar when news arrived that Admiral Nelson had died at the battle of Trafalgar. Other curiosities include a complete suit of armour!

Unusual interior!

▶ White Lion Inn at a glance

Open: Mon–Sun 12noon–11.00pm

Brewery/company: Free house

Real ales: Wainwrights, Windermere Brewing Company, guest beers

Food: Daily 12noon–2pm, 6–9pm.

Rooms: Five rooms en-suite

Outside: Beer garden

Children & dogs: Children welcome. Muddy boots and Dogs welcome

The Walk

1. Turn right out of the car park and walk along the road. Take the signed right of way along a **farm track** ('Howtown, Side Farm') beside the **George Starkey Hut**. Follow the track across the valley floor, through the **farmyard**, past the tearoom and turn left after the farm buildings along a wide track. Immediately after a wide gate across the track, turn right up by a wall to join a broad footpath.

Turn left along this path soon passing

mine remains on the right and an **old iron seat** *(there is a great view from this seat across the head of lake to the Helvellyn range).*

2. In around half a mile an obvious grassy footpath forks right (at this point you should be able to see the village of Glenridding across the lake between two stands of pines). Bear right onto this path to begin your climb to the summit. As the path climbs it becomes steeper and rockier but remains straightforward to follow.

Where the angle eventually eases the path swings right. Just before it levels out, bear right at a fork. This path weaves through boggy hollows and between small rocky knolls to eventually reach the **summit of Place Fell**.

Despite its modest height, Place Fell provides one of the best viewpoints in the eastern fells with Ullswater wrapped around the fell's lower slopes.

3. Cross the summit (maked by a stone trig pillar) and take the broad footpath

![Looking down to Ullswater and Glenridding from Place Fell]

Looking down to Ullswater and Glenridding from Place Fell

ahead (heading south) with Red Screes and Brothers Water directly ahead. The path is well worn and easy to follow and becomes steeper as you descend to eventually reach **Boredale Hause**, the broad saddle separating Boredale from Patterdale.

4. Take the path to the right here keeping right and taking a diagonal line down the fellside aiming for Patterdale village down in the valley.

Cross the stream and go through a gate on the right. Turn left now and follow the **lane** back across the valley floor, to cross the river and join the main road. Turn right along the road. The **White Lion** is on the right, the car park is a little further on. ◆

Red deer

Place Fell and Martindale are home to one of the oldest native herds of red deer in England. Now protected on the Dalemain Estate, there have been red deer around Ullswater for at least 300 years. Climb the hills at dawn or dusk during the mating season in October and November, and you're likely to hear the stags' noisy mating calls as they fight over breeding females.

Enjoying an outdoor drink at The Britannia Inn

The Britannia Inn | Lingmoor Fell Elterwater

Distance/time: 7km / 4½ miles. Allow 2½–3 hours

Start: Official car park in the centre of Elterwater opposite The Britannia Inn.

Grid ref: NY 328 048

Ordnance Survey Map: OL 7 The English Lakes South-eastern area. *Windermere, Kendal & Silverdale*

The Pub: The Britannia Inn, Elterwater, Ambleside LA22 9HP | 015394 37210 | www.thebritanniainn.com| info@britinn.co.uk

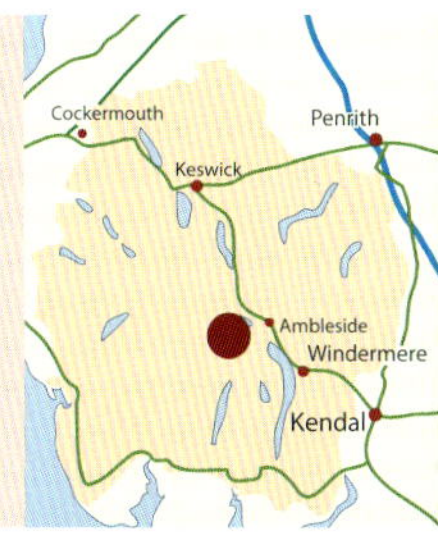

Walk outline: Leaving the village of Elterwater by an old lane, the route heads steeply onto the open fell. The broad, rollowing ridge is then followed to the rocky summit with its stunning views of the Langdale Pikes. Return is made via the northern slopes and Baysbrown Wood where the local slate mines are still in operation.

The Britannia Inn is possibly one of the best known and and best loved pubs in Cumbria. The building is thought to date back almost 500 years and has been a pub since at least the late 1800s when it served local quarrymen and workers from the nearby gun powder factory which closed in 1929.

▶ The Britannia Inn at a glance

Open: Daily 11am–11pm
Brewery/company: Free house
Real ales: A range of real ales from Langdale Brewing Company as well as regular guest beers from Coniston Brewery beers
Food: Lunch is served from 12–2pm, Soup and Sandwiches 2–4pm and Dinner 5.30–8.30pm.
Rooms: A selection of double and twin rooms which all offer either a private bathroom or en-suite facilities
Outside: Spacious beer garden
Children & dogs: Both welcome to dine or stay

The Walk

1. Turn left out of the car park, cross the **bridge** and pass the **Hostel**. Bear right along a lane in around 200 metres just beyond the entrance to 'The Eltermere Inn'. Pass **Eltermere Hall** and where the lane bends right, keep ahead on a rough untarmaced road signed to 'Little Langdale'. The track is stony and rises steadily through woods.

This is one of many old fell lanes which never became motorable (probably because of the steepness) and have remained unmetalled. They now provide ideal traffic-free walking and off-road cycle routes.

2. As you emerge from the woods keep ahead at a footpath junction with the graceful contours of Wetherlam (one of the Coniston fells) rising ahead. In another 200 metres or so, where the track levels, look for a **footgate** and footpath on the right (before you reach a farm on the left).

Go through the gate and swing diagonally left on a good footpath passing through a second **gate**.

Continue rising to another **gate** leading onto the open fell. A good footpath

Lingmoor Fell rising above the village of Elterwater

zig-zags up the steep hillside eventually easing as you gain the ridge.

The path continues more or less along the broad ridge crest, never straying far from the **wall** on the right.

Note the **metal gate** in the wall for the descent.

Pass a **stone seat** with views back to Windermere and Elterwater. The path is easy to follow rising over minor tops and dips along the watershed but remaining close to the **wall/fence** on the right.

Swing right with the wall/fence making a final rise to the **summit of Lingmoor Fell** accessed by a **stile** on the right.

Like many smaller fells, Lingmoor stands apart from its neighbours and thus makes an excellet viewpoint. The view takes in the Langdale Pikes, Bowfell, Esk Pike, Pike 'o Blisco, Wetherlam and the Fairfield group.

3. Retrace your steps back along the ridge to the **metal gate** in the wall on the left noted earlier. Go through the gate and follow the well worn path down through scattered, stunted **yew trees**, zig-zaging lower down to a footpath T junction.

Looking across to the Langdale Pikes from Lingmoor Fell

Turn right here signed to 'Elterwater, Langdale'. The path soon passes through disussed **mine workings**, then woods to reach a lane.

4. Turn left, then right almost immediately signed to 'Chapel Stile, Elterwater'. Follow a gravel footpath through **quarry workings**. Cross the quarry road continuing the descent past **cottages** on the right to eventually join **a riverside path**.

The area around Great Langdale and Little Langdale has a long history of quarrying with Elterwater Quarry being one of the largest. This quarry has been worked since approximately the middle of the 19th century. Stone is still extracted here with permission to continue production well in to the 2040s.

Proposals have recently been put forward by the current owners, Burlington Stone, to turn the quarry and adjacent mines into a complex visitor attraction similar to the ones at Honister near Buttermere and Bleanau Ffestiniog in Snowdonia, with zip wires and underground tours, but there has been a great deal of local opposition. Opposers of the plans fear the nearby villages of Elterwater and Chapel Stile will be unable to cope with the huge increase in traffic and visitor numbers.

5. Just before a **footbridge** on the left, bear right signed for 'Elterwater, Ambleside'. Follow the path beside the river to eventually join the **quarry access road**. Turn left and follow the road back to Elterwater where a left turn over the bridge brings you back to the car park to complete the walk. ♦

Norse origins

Cumbria is rich in Norse place name elements with 'dale' from 'dalr' meaning a valley and 'fell' from 'fjall' meaning mountain or large hill, being the most common. Other common place name elements include; 'bekkr'—a stream from which we get 'beck', 'tjorn'—a small lake giving us the uniquely Lakeland word 'tarn', and 'fors/foss'—a waterfall, appearing as 'force' a name common throughout Cumbria and Yorkshire.

The Riverside Bar, Scafell Hotel

The Riverside Bar | Grange Fell Borrowdale

Distance/time: 10km/6 miles. Allow 3–3½ hours

Start: National Trust's Bowder Stone car park in Borrowdale

Grid ref: NY 253 168

Ordnance Survey Map: Explorer OL 4 The English Lakes *Northwestern area. Keswick, Cockermouth & Wigton*

The Pub: The Riverside Bar, Scafel Hotel, Rosthwaite, Borrowdale, Cumbria CA12 5XB | 017687 77208 | www.scafell.co.uk

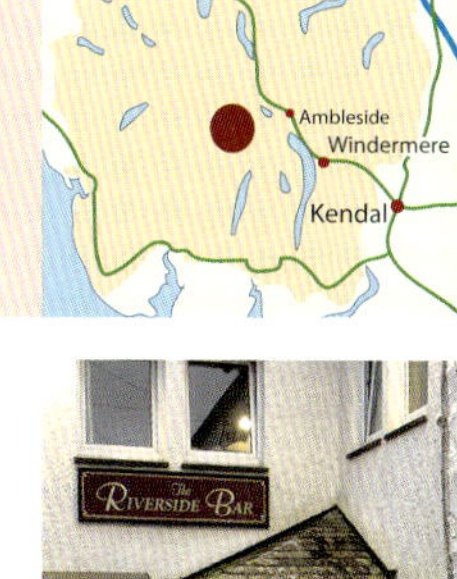

Walk outline: A steep climb through woods is followed by two open summits with fine views. This is followed by a straight forward descent into Borrowdale for a break at The Riverside Bar in Rosthwaite. A more leisurely return is made by following the Cumbria Way beside the River Derwent.

The Riverside Bar is a straight forward walkers' bar situated to the rear of the Scafell Hotel in Rosthwaite, overlooking the river. Its large single baroom has an open fire and plenty of seating with real ale and bar snacks served each day. Muddy boots and dogs are welcome.

The Riverside Bar

▶ The Riverside Bar at a glance

Open: Daily Mon–Sat 12noon–11pm; Sun 12noon–10.30pm

Brewery/company: Freehouse

Real ales: Tirril Borrowdale Bitter, Tirril Old Faithful

Food: Daily 12 noon–2pm; evenings 6pm–9pm

Rooms: 23 rooms available in the adjacent hotel (www.scafell.co.uk)

Outside: No outside seating

Children & dogs: Children welcome and dogs allowed on flagged area of the bar

The Walk

1. From the top parking area (immediately above the picnic benches), walk over to the far side of the car park and you will see a **small wooden gate** in the corner of fence below. Go through the gate and follow the narrow footpath ahead soon passing a **large boulder** on the right. Pass through a small, **disused quarry** and continue climbing gently through more open ground. The path swings right through an area of bracken and light birch wood.

2. The path levels beside a **large boulder** on the right with a **stone wall** ahead. Go through a gate in the wall, following a path that drops a little, then bear right ignoring a path to a gate on the left. The path crosses a stream, then rises up through the trees.

At a T junction (with a wall and stile down to the left) turn right to begin the climb to **King's How**. The path is **pitched** as the slope steepens making the going much easier than it would othereise be.

Eventually the angle eases and the path is almost level before swinging right and steepening again. Skirt a **boggy area** to the right and pass beneath a solitary yew tree. Beyond the tree, the path rises, rocky at first, through young birch trees curving around the fell with occasional glimpses of **Derwent Water** through the trees far below.

A final climb and you emerge on the summit of **King's How**, with it's stunning views of Derwent Water and Skiddaw.

Crossing 'New Bridge' over the River Derwent

3. Grange Fell, the next summit and the highest point on the walk, is clearly visible as one of the rocky knolls over to the east. You can also see the path cutting eastwards over boggy ground.

Leave the summit on the path that initially heads south, in the direction of Rosthwaite (visible down in the valley below). At a fork keep left, then bear left again between rocks to reach a boggy saddle with a stile in the fence ahead. Cross this stile and follow the narrow but visible footpath ahead.

Cross a stile over a stone wall and continue for around 250 metres. Look for a cairn on the left marking the path to the the next summit.

4. Turn left here to reach the summit of Grange Fell. There a number of small rocky summits and it's not immediately obvious which one is the highest.

Take the grassy path that heads down the gentle southern slopes (to the right as you approached the summit). Cross the stile in the fence corner and continue to reach the broad path connecting Watendlath and Rosthwaite.

5. Turn right and follow the path down

The stunning view to Derwent Water from King's How

into Borrowdale. Ignore a gate to the right lower down, continuing to cross a bridge over the beck.

Much lower down turn right through a gate on the signed bridleway to 'Rosthwaite'. The path continues to descend eventually reaching the entrance to 'Hazel Bank' on the left. Turn right over the bridge and follow the lane down to the road. Turn left into Rosthwaite. **The Riverside Bar** is part of the **Scafell Hotel**. The bar entrance is at the back of the hotel on the left.

6. Leaving the bar, turn right and take the first road on the left. At the end of the lane, walk through the **farmyard** and continue along a track. The track curves to the right and runs alongside the **River Derwent** to the **stone-built** '**New Bridge**'.

Cross the bridge, turn right and continue beside the river on a path shared by the **Cumbria Way**. A little further on the path swings to the left, away from the river. Ignore a path on the left here keeping ahead to soon enter **High Hows Wood**.

Initially the path stays close to the river. Pass **small quarry workings** and at a fork, take a sharp right. Soon you are beside the river again. Continue to reach a T-junction with a track near

a **campsite**. Turn right here and at the end of the track, turn right again following a tarmac lane into the tiny village of **Grange**.

Cross the **old stone bridge** over the River Derwent and turn right along the road. Take care on this section. Follow the road for about 700 metres to reach the car park on the left to complete the walk. ♦

The Bowder Stone

Perhaps Lakeland's most famous rock, this 2,000-ton stone, is 30 feet high and 50 feet across and is a relic of the region's glacial past. Unusually, it was not carried into the area by ice but toppled into its present position from the crags above. This happened after the glacier that once filled Borrowdale retreated and no longer supported the steep side of the valley, resulting in huge rock falls.

Woolpack Inn, Hardknott Bar & Café

Woolpack Inn | Harter Fell
Eskdale

Distance/time: 11km / 6½ miles. Allow 3½–4 hours

Start: Limited parking is available at the foot of the Hardknott Pass, Eskdale

Grid ref: NY 210 011

Ordnance Survey Map: OL 6 The English Lakes South-western area. *Coniston, Ulverston & Barrow-in-Furness*

The Pub: Woolpack Inn, Hardknott Bar & Café, Hardknott Pass, Eskdale, Cumbria CA19 1TH | 01946 723 230 | www.woolpack.co.uk

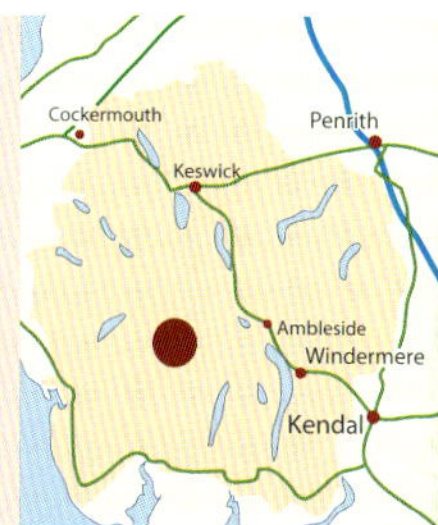

Walk outline: Beginning at the foot of the Hardknott Pass—the UK's steepest road, the walk takes you up past the Hardknott Roman Fort before heading up onto the open fellside. An increasingly rocky ascent leads to the superb summit of this miniture mountain with stunning views. An equally steep rocky descent leads back to the valley, with a return along a quiet lane.

The Hardknott Bar & Café is part of the Woolpack Inn—a welcoming traditional walker's bar in a beautiful, largely unspoilt rural setting at the foot of the famous Hardknott Pass. A range of local ales and food are on offer daily.

▶ Woolpack Inn, Hardknott Bar & Cafe

Open: Daily 8am–11pm

Brewery/company: Free house

Real ales: Range of local real ales

Food: Open daily for breakfast 8am–12noon; lunch 12noon–3pm dinner 5pm–8pm. Pizza available 5pm–8pm & 12noon–9pm weekends

Rooms: Fourteen en-suite rooms

Outside: Larger garden area in sunny location with tables, chairs and fire pit

Children & dogs: Both welcome to dine or stay

The Walk

1. From the parking area head towards the **Hardknott Pass**. Beyond the **cattle grid** the road rises steeply. At the edge of woods on the left turn left, cross a ladder stile and turn right immediately on a footpath that heads directly up the hillside through bracken. Higher up squeeze through an **tiny gateway** in the wall and continue on the obvious path climbing directly up to the remains of the **Roman fort**.

Pass through the **lower entrance** and walk through the fort (*see the box on page 57*). Leave by the opposite entrance taking the faint grassy path ahead. This rises directly at first, then curves right beneath the steeper scree-covered slopes to eventually reach the road on one of the tight hairpin bends.

Follow the road left up to the top of the pass. *The Hardknott Pass is renown for being the steepest road in Britain.*

2. As you near the **summit of the pass** the angle eases. Before you reach the highest point, look for **abroad footpath** on the right. This looks like it could almost be a rough 4x4 track at first. Turn right a follow this path. Within 100 metres or so the path forks—bear right here. Pass the corner of a **ruined stone wall** on the left. Harter Fell comes into view soon and the ground is marshy with a **fence** to the right. Keep ahead in the direction of the pointed Harter Fell and very shortly a **small pool** is visible

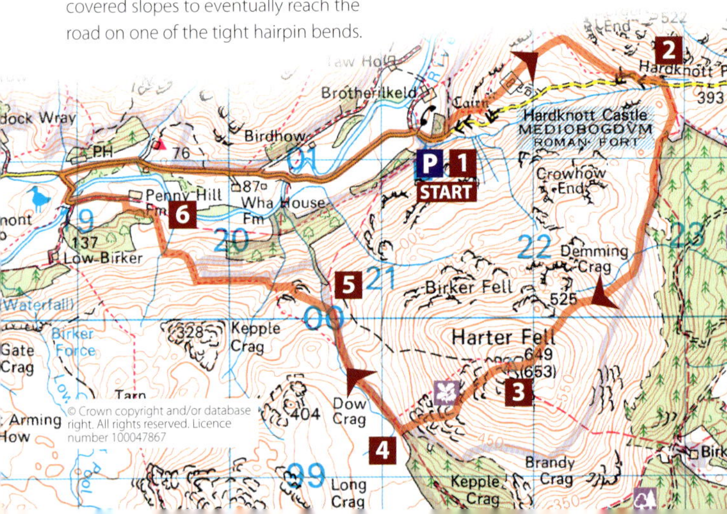

Harter Fell rising above the remains of the Hard Knott Roman Fort

over to the right. Keep ahead, cross a stile over the fence and bear left.

A good footpath soon establishes itself running roughly parallel to the **fence** over to the left and never out of sight of it. The path makes a slight drop into a marshy hollow. Keep ahead, still in sight of the fence on the left and heading for a stile ahead, but to the right of the fence corner where there is also a stile.

The ground rises more steeply now and the path climbs more or less directly heading for the pointed summit of **Harter Fell** which remains visible for most the ascent now. It's a head down slog up marshy ground for a while and you will encounter a number of paths. All the ascending paths have the same goal however, so the choice is yours.

With no close neighbours, Harter Fell offers a fine view in all directions but your attention will most likely to be drawn by the view north to the Scafell group.

3. From the summit, take the path which heads southwest in the direction of Sellafield and the large lake visible on the moors (Devoke Water), dropping steeply between rocky knolls. **Woods**

The spectacular view towards the Scafell group from the summit

are soon visible below. The path heads for the right-hand end of the woods where it meets the footpath crossing the broad marshy saddle.

4. Turn right along this path. In around 500 metres or so, and before you get a clear view into Eskdale, there is a **ruined stone wall** beyond the fence on your left. Continue until immediately before a tiny stream crosses the path and the ruined wall on the left turns left.

5. Turn left here crossing a stile over the fence. The path follows the wall until (in around 75-100 metres) there is a **gap in the wall** (ignore the footpath ahead here). Go left through the gap to cross the **stream**. The path follows the edge of a **small gorge** now on the right.

Cross a stile in the fence and soon descend more steeply beside the fence. Bear left at the bottom of the slope and cross the **stream** by an **oak tree**. The path continues beside a **well bulit stone** wall with views into Eskdale.

Eventually the wall turns right and the path turns with it, heading steeply down to a **gate** in the corner. Through the gate, the the path becomes better defined as you descend becoming a rough farm track. After two large gates the track eventually swings left towards a **farm**.

6. Before the next gate into the farm, bear left on a signed **permitted path**. Through a small footgate the path follows a high wall before turning right through a second gate and over a small field to join the access road.

Turn left and follow the access road over the **River Esk** to reach the main lane through the valley. A right turn here will take you shortly to the **Woolpack Inn**. Continue along the lane to complete the walk. ◆

Hardknott Roman Fort

The substantial remains of the Roman Hardknott Fort sit high on a grassy spur above Eskdale. Built originally in the second century by Emperor Hadrian, the fort housed 500 infantry soldiers from what are now the Balkan countries of Croatia, Bosnia-Herzogovina and Montegnegro. Their tricky task was to guard the high, wind-swept road over Hardknott Pass from the fierce local Brigantes tribe. The fort was abandoned only a century later.

Wasdale Head Inn

Wasdale Head Inn
Scafell Pike | Wasdale

Distance/time: 14.5km / 8¾ miles. Allow 3–4 hours

Start: Large parking area at Wasdale Green, about 400 metres before the Wasdale Head Inn

Grid ref: NY 186 084

Ordnance Survey Map: OL 6 The English Lakes South-western area. *Coniston, Ulverston & Barrow-in-Furness*

The Pub: Wasdale Head Inn, Wasdale Head, Near Gosforth, Cumbria CA20 1EX | reception@wasdale.com | (019467) 26229

Walk outline: From Wasdale Head this route heads up to Sty Head pass and the high saddle of Esk Hause. From there the path climbs up onto the summit plateau—the highest ridgeline in the Lake District. Spectacular views in all directions can be enjoyed in clear conditions before the descent over Lingmell and its broad west ridge.

The Wasdale Head Inn is famous as the place where the sport of rock climbing begain in the late 19th century. Today this large hotel and bar retains its traditional charm with images from of its famous past lining the walls and rooms named after many of the famous pioneer rock climbers.

Wasdale Head Inn

▶ Wasdale Head Inn at a glance

Open: Mon–Sat, 11am–11pm; Sun 12noon–11pm

Brewery/company: Free house

Real ales: Seven regular changing ales including beers from Cumbrian Brewing Company and Cumbrian Legendary Ales

Food: Daily, 12noon–8.30pm

Rooms: 9 rooms in the hotel, plus 7 selfcatering appartments in adjacent barn conversions

Outside: Outside seating and tables

Children & dogs: Children and dogs both welcome

The Walk

1. From the northern end of the **green** take the walled farm lane beside 'Lingmell House'. This leads between the small walled-fields which are so characteristic of Wasdale Head, past the tiny **church of Saint Olaf** to **Burnthwaite Farm**. Bear left as signed immediately before the farm and pass between the outbuildings to continue on a good path with the commanding prospect of Great Gable rising ahead.

The bridleway crosses a **footbridge** over **Gable Beck**, then runs tight below the long southern slopes of the mountain beside the tumbling **Lingmell Beck**. At a fork, keep left on the higher path.

As you climb higher the impressive prow of Lingmell, the final summit of the day, rears up across the valley and there are impressive views looking back to the handfull of buildings at Wasdale Head.

2. *Sty Head* pass is the meeting of many routes. Old pack horse trails linking Wasdale with Borrowdale and Langdale, used this high pass and you will often see tents beside Sty Head Tarn. The high point of the pass is marked by a large boulder and **mountain rescue box**. Take the path on the right here which climbs gently to **Sprinkling Tarn**, another popular camping spot cradled in a grassy hollow.

The path ahead continues the moderate climb to **Esk Hause**, 1km/¾ mile distant and famous for lying at the very centre of the Lakeland fells. In the approach to the hause bear right at a fork (the

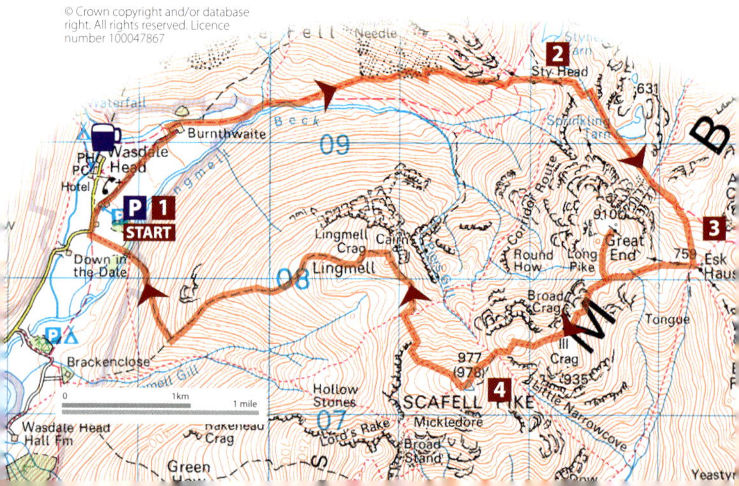

Starting the descent to Lingmell with Great Gable beyond

left fork leads to a slightly lower pass separating Esk Hause from the summit of Allen Crags.

Esk Hause lies at the head of upper Esk Dale one of the wildest and most remote valleys in the Lake District and surrounded by Lakeland's highest fells. In clear conditions its impressive setting can be appreciated fully—Esk Pike and Bowfell on the left and the impressive Ill Crag—one of Scafell Pike's satellites—on the right.

3. Turn right here on the path which leads up through the little hollow of **Calf Cove** and onto the broad ridge.

Turn right for **Great End**, 300-400m north across the plateau. *Predictably, it is a superb viewpoint, particularly for Great Gable and Wasdale Head, but also for the castellated crags of Lingmell. You can also see the entire route from here—the broad rocky ridge linking Great End with Scafell Pike, along with the outliers of Ill Crag and Broad Crag.*

Retrace your steps, then follow the broad path southwest. Straightforward enough in clear conditions, less so in the mist, although there are frequent cairns and the path is well worn.

The view into the remote upper Eskdale from ill Crag

The main path bypasses the summits of **Ill Crag** and **Broad Crag**, both requiring short detours.

Make sure you don't miss the pointed summit of Ill Crag—this top is worth the detour mainly for the stunning view down the mountain's southern face into the wilds of upper Esk Dale, the snaking river seen against the impressive rock summit of Pen. It also provides a better resting place than Scafell Pike as the latter attracts the crowds and can be a busy spot even on the quietest of days.

Beyond Broad Crag a drop to the little pass at the head of **Little Narrowcove** followed by a short scrambly ridge and

you are on the **highest summit in England**.

4. From Scafell Pike take the good cairned footpath which heads northwest. Ignore the path which soon breaks away left. This leads to **Mickledore** and Scafell.

The path descends to **Lingmell Col** before the rise to the final summit of the day. The **broad Hollow Stones** path breaks away left here which can used if time is pressing, otherwise continue ahead up the ridge to Lingmell, an easy 100m rise.

Descend by the path which heads west

for about 1km/¾ mile to join the steep, rounded grassy ridge which drops beside Lingmell Gill. Don't descend all the way to the gill, instead take the path which strikes rightwards about halfway down the ridge to make a diagonal descent of the hillside to the **footbridge** over **Lingmell Beck**. Cross the bridge and follow the path ahead back to Wasdale Green to complete the route. ♦

The birth of rock climbing

Wasdale Head is where rock climbing as a sport began with the ascent of the famous Napes Needle, a 20-metre high rock pinnacle on the flanks of Great Gable, in 1886. The first ascent was made by Walter Parry Haskett-Smith who is said to have celebrated his achievement by standing on his head on the very top! Although the original route used is quite modest by modern standards it still graded 'hard severe' in modern guidebooks.

Useful Information

Cumbria Tourism

Cumbria Tourism's official website covers everything from accommodation and events to attractions and adventure. **www.golakes.co.uk**

Lake District National Park

The Lake District National Park website also has information on things to see and do, plus maps, webcams and news. **www.lakedistrict.gov.uk**

Tourist Information Centres

The main TICs provide free information on everything from accommodation and travel to what's on and walking advice.

Ambleside	01539 432 582	tic@thehubofambleside.com
Bowness	01539 442 895	bownesstic@lakedistrict.gov.uk
Coniston	01539 441 533	mail@conistontic.org
Keswick	01768 772 645	keswicktic@lakedistrict.gov.uk
Penrith	01768 867 466	pen.tic@eden.gov.uk
Ullswater	01768 482 414	ullswatertic@lakedistrict.gov.uk
Windermere	01539 446 499	info@windermereinfo.co.uk

Cumbrian breweries and pubs

As well as the mainstream Cumbrian breweries such as Jennings, the Lake District supports more than twenty micro-breweries producing award-winning real ales and craft beers, plus five real cider and perry makers.

For details of the encouragingly high number of real ale pubs in the Lake District, see the local CAMRA websites, or buy a copy of their excellent, annual *Good Beer Guide*.

Visitors can also sample a mouth-watering range of local real ales at the many Lakeland beer festivals held throughout the year.

See: **www.camra.org.uk** or **www.cumbriacamra.org.uk**

Weather

Five-day forecast for the Lake District

0844 846 2444 | **www.lakedistrict.gov.uk/visiting/weather-enjoying**